THE BOOK OF BAD BETTI

Vanessa Kisuule is a writer and performer based in Bristol. She has been featured on BBC iPlayer, Radio 1, and Radio 4's Woman's Hour, Blue Peter, Don't Flop and TEDx in Vienna. Her poem on the historic toppling of Edward Colston's statue 'Hollow' gained over 600,000 views on Twitter in three days. She has two poetry collections published by Burning Eye Books and her work was Highly Commended in the Forward Poetry Prize Anthology 2019. She has written for The Guardian, NME and Lonely Planet and toured her one woman show 'SEXY' in 2017. She was the Bristol City Poet 2018 - 2020 and is working on an essay collection and her debut novel.

Anja Konig grew up in the German language and now writes in English. Her first collection, *Animal Experiments*, was published by Bad Betty Press in 2020. Her first pamphlet *Advice for an Only Child*, from flipped eye, was shortlisted for the 2015 Michael Marks prize.

Gale Acuff has had poetry published in *Ascent, Reed, Poet Lore, Chiron Review, Cardiff Review, Poem, Adirondack Review, Florida Review, Slant, Nebo, Arkansas Review, South Dakota Review, Roanoke Review,* and many other journals in a dozen countries. Gale has authored three books of poetry: *Buffalo Nickel, The Weight of the World,* and *The Story of My Lives.*

Polly Atkin lives in Cumbria. Her first poetry collection *Basic Nest Architecture* (Seren: 2017) is followed by *Much With Body* (Seren: 2021) and a biography *Recovering Dorothy: The Hidden Life of Dorothy Wordsworth* (Saraband: 2021). She is working on a memoir exploring place, belonging and disability.

Erdem Avsar (he/him) is a writer of plays, poems, and essays. Queering conventional forms, he explores socio-political issues around queer migration, human rights, and urban poverty. He is an affiliate artist at UNESCO RILA, and the 2019 recipient of the Kevin Elyot Award. His plays have been shown in Scotland, Turkey, and Italy. He is a PhD researcher at the University of Glasgow where he explores queer politics and LGBTQI+ performance in Turkey.

Honey Baxter is a poet and novelist from Gloucestershire with degrees in Creative Writing and Writing for Young People from Bath Spa University. Their work is informed by desire, pop culture, and the body.

Chloe Bettles writes about mental health in a (hopefully) humorous way. She is currently studying for a masters in poetry at the University of East Anglia. Her poetic debut was as part of the winning slam team at UniSlam 2019 where she was later longlisted for the Out-Spoken Prize for Poetry.

K. Blair (she/they) is bisexual, bigender and biding their time on Twitter: @WhattheBlair, and Instagram: @urban_barbarian. They are a member of London Queer Writers and host of SPEAK =. She recently took a quiz on 'what horror trope are you?' and is very smug that she got 'Final Girl'.

Laurie Bolger is a London based writer. Her work has featured at Glastonbury, TATE, Sky Arts and across various BBC platforms. Laurie is the founder of *The Creative Writing Breakfast Club* featured in Time Out. She is working on her second book *Call Me Lady*.

Helen Bowell is London-based poet and co-director of Dead [Women] Poets Society. She is a Ledbury Poetry Critic, and an alumna of The Writing Squad and the Roundhouse Poetry Collective. Her debut pamphlet is forthcoming from Bad Betty Press. She works at The Poetry Society.

Helen Bowie (she/her/they/them) is a writer, performer and charity worker based in London. Their debut pamphlet, *WORD/PLAY* will be published by Beir Bua Press in 2021. She loves cats, and mayonnaise and hates injustice and ketchup. Helen is Extremely Online at twitter.com/helensulis.

Troy Cabida (he/him) is a Filipino poet, creative producer and librarian from south-west London. His recent poems appear in *harana poetry*, *bath magg*, *MacMillan* and the Roundhouse. His debut pamphlet, *War Dove*, was published by Bad Betty Press in May 2020. He also serves as producer for London open mic night *Poetry and Shaah*.

Jemima Foxtrot is a writer and performer from Yorkshire living in Berlin and London. She has written and toured several works for the stage to critical acclaim. Her second collection of poetry, *A New Game*, will be published in 2022 by Burning Eye Books.

Jasmine Gray is a Northern writer, interested in exploring the female experience and portrayals of the body. A Writing Squad graduate, she has art criticism published in *TILT* (2021) and forthcoming with The Double Negative. Her debut poetry pamphlet, *Let's Photograph Girls Enjoying Life*, is published with Broken Sleep (2019).

Fee Griffin's debut collection, *For Work / For TV*, was published in December 2020 by Versal Editions and won the inaugural Amsterdam Open Book Prize. She is a senior poetry editor at *The Lincoln Review* and has recent work published in *Poetry London*, *bath magg*, *SAND*, *Streetcake*, *Peach Mag* and other journals. She works part time as an associate lecturer, part time for SO Festival and part time as a cleaner.

Marguerite Harrold's poems thread the ecology of being human through urban and rural landscapes, to explore the ways we connect to place, dislocation and to one another. Marguerite was nominated for the 2020 Pushcart Prize and a 2020 grant from the Illinois Arts Council, was a 2020 Finalist for an Allied Arts grant, and is a member of the Community of Writers at Squaw Valley. Marguerite is recently retired from Chicago Department of Public Health, after 20 years of service in HIV Prevention and Environmental Health.

Julie Irigaray is a French Basque poet living in the UK. Her début pamphlet *Whalers, Witches and Gauchos* was published by Nine Pens Press in April 2021. Her poems have appeared internationally in *Ambit Magazine*, *Magma*, *Stand* and *Mslexia*. She was commended in the 2020 Ambit Magazine Poetry Prize; shortlisted for The White Review Poet's Prize 2019, and selected as one of the 50 Best New British and Irish Poets 2018 (Eyewear Publishing).

Safiya Kamaria Kinshasa is a British born Barbadian raised poet of Jamaican and Barbadian descent. Using her background in dance and cultural studies, her poetry chiefly encompasses dance on the page and stage. Safiya's first collection will be released with Out-Spoken Press. Safiya is a recipient of the inaugural Jerwood Arts | Apples & Snakes Poetry in Performance Programme. In 2020, she was awarded the New Voice in Poetry Prize, and shortlisted for the Out-Spoken Prize for Poetry and The Creative Future Writers' Award.

Cecilia Knapp is the Young People's Laureate for London, 2020-2021. She curated the poetry anthology *Everything is going to be Alright* (Trapeze.) She was shortlisted for the 2020 Rebecca Swift Women's Prize. Her debut novel *Little Boxes* (The Borough Press) and her collection *Peach Pig* (Corsair) are forthcoming in 2022.

Jill Michelle teaches at Valencia College in Orlando, Florida. Her poetry and creative nonfiction have appeared or are forthcoming in *The Cypress Dome*, *The Fox Hat Review*, *Wizards in Space*, *Please See Me*, *86Logic*, *The Tule Review*, *Paper Dragon*, *Halfway Down the Stairs* and *Prospectus*.

Jenny Mitchell is the winner of the Ware Poetry Prize 2021, the Folklore Prize 2020 and several other competitions. She has been nominated for a Forward Prize and a debut collection, *Her Lost Language*, was voted One of 44 Books of 2019 (Poetry Wales). Her latest collection is *Map of a Plantation* (Indigo Dreams).

Charlotte Newbury is a poet from South East England with an MA in Creative Writing from the University of Exeter. She likes witchcraft, ecofeminism and spider plants. Her writing has appeared or is forthcoming in *LandLocked*, *Perhappened*, *Burning Jade* and others. You can find her on twitter @charnewbpoet.

Madeleine Pulman-Jones is a poet, writer, and translator. Her poems have appeared in publications including *PN Review* and *The Adroit Journal*, where she was a finalist for the 2020 Adroit Prize for Poetry. She recently received the Harper-Wood Creative Writing and Travel Award for English Poetry and Literature from St. John's College, Cambridge. The award will fund a year in Barcelona, where she will work on a collection of poems.

Ellora Sutton, 24, is a queer poet from Hampshire. She has won the Mslexia Poetry Competition, the Poetry Society and Artlyst's Art to Poetry Award, and the Pre-Raphaelite Society Poetry Competition. She has been published by *Poetry Birmingham Literary Journal*, *Poetry News*, *Ink Sweat & Tears*, and *fourteen poems*, amongst others. She tweets @ellora_sutton.

Ojo Taiye is a young Nigerian who uses poetry as a handy tool to write his frustration with society. He also makes use of collage and sampling techniques.

Claudine Toutoungi's collections *Smoothie* (2017) and *Two Tongues* (2020) are published by Carcanet Press. Her poems have appeared in *Poetry*, *The Poetry Review*, *PN Review*, *The Guardian*, *The New Statesman*, *Poetry London*, *Poetry Ireland Review* and elsewhere. Claudine's plays for radio and stage include *Slipping*, *Deliverers* and *The Inheritors*.

Christian Yeo is a final-year Singaporean law undergraduate. His work has been published or is forthcoming in *The Mays*, *Anthropocene*, *Quarterly Literary Review Singapore*, *Ekstasis Magazine*, *The Tiger Moth Review*, *Notes*, *6'98*, *The Dial*, and *the jfa human rights journal*, among others; won the Arthur Sale Poetry Prize, and was longlisted for the Sykes Prize and Lumiere Review Poetry Prize. His work has been performed at the Lancaster and Singapore Poetry Festivals, and he was a semi-finalist at UniSlam 2021.

THE BOOK OF BAD BETTIES

BAD BETTY PRESS

The Book of Bad Betties

Published by Bad Betty Press in 2021
www.badbettypress.com

Vanessa Kisuule and Anja Konig have asserted their right to be identified as the editors of this work in accordance with Section 77 of the Copyright, Designs and Patents Act of 1988.

Cover design by Helen Nicholson

Printed and bound in the United Kingdom

A CIP record of this book is available from the British Library.

ISBN: 978-1-913268-23-7

Supported using public funding by
ARTS COUNCIL ENGLAND
LOTTERY FUNDED

The Book of Bad Betties

Edited by Vanessa Kisuule and Anja Konig

Contents

I CAN BE A SHOW PONY

BESEECH THE SKY

What Is a Bad Betty?
Editors in conversation

Vanessa Kisuule: So I think if you'd asked me this, let's say five years ago—really peak time for the latest wave of what we're now starting to understand as neoliberal feminism—there was a lot of 'boss bitch', 'girl boss' type stuff going around. It was the era of Beyoncé using the term feminist and Chimamanda's speech and I had a very particular idea of what a Bad Betty was in that particular time. And it was quite glossy and shiny. It was about being strong in the performative way, probably represented by someone in a pair of thigh-high boots doing lots of kicks, which speaks a lot to the images of girl power that I grew up with, which is people like the Spice Girls. And now I feel a bit embarrassed because I don't think being a Bad Betty is about that. I *love* those things, but I think being a Bad Betty is a much quieter and less performative thing, and the poems that moved me most weren't about women that were powerful or strong in those more obvious ways.

Anja Konig: Yeah, I was thinking a lot about this. There is an element of strength. Sometimes strength is just surviving and not breaking. And a lot of the poems that were moving were celebrating survival in a system that is still hostile. So a Bad Betty is coming from a place where they are an underdog in some ways. A Bad Betty isn't somebody who's entitled by the system to a position of power but attains a position of strength, through their Bad Betty-ness which is…

VK: …that's the thing that's hard to define, right?

AK: They're not broken, you know. But then, why shouldn't somebody be a Bad Betty who *is* broken? Because in some ways we are all broken.

13

VK: I love the idea of unruliness. And again, not necessarily in that Lara Croft, badass woman with abs way, and more just messy, irritable, tired, stretched thin. Most of the women I know are all of those things. But as you say, they don't break, they persevere, sometimes they get very close to breaking, but they don't. And the poems that moved me were the ones that acknowledged those complexities. Because a lot of them were writing about people that are close to them; there was that deep sense of knowledge and observation, of looking at someone you love: the tiny gestures and moments of softness and vulnerability. And also the moments of humour, of insouciance, of cheekiness and I think *that* unruliness—to be all of those things in a world that wants you sanitised and constantly smiling and appeasing people—is definitely what makes a Bad Betty to me. I think, for all the progress we've made as a society, there's still lots of ways that we are punished as women, or non-binary people, for not accommodating, for not trying to please everybody all the time.

AK: ....punished for not being in the box, so Bad Betty-ness does have an element of subversion. The kind of subversion that's necessary for survival, if you are defined to be inside the box.

VK: Which is ironic because that very subversion can sometimes be the thing that puts you in danger. It would be remiss to not acknowledge that a lot of people toe the line and do what society asks of them because they feel that that's safer. A lot of women look at the world around them and they say—okay, am I gonna constantly push against these rules and regulations, or am I going to sit here, be quiet, be amenable? And it makes perfect sense why a lot of women choose the latter, because society has and does punish women who go against that, but I agree with you that there's something on the other side of that for the women that do survive those transgressions.

AK: And we are all these things at the same time. Even somebody who is a fighter, sometimes, may decide to let some dogs lie. Even if you're a fighter on some issues on some days, there are the days you're just too fucking tired.

VK: And I think a lot of the poems touch on that too: the disappointments, the moments where you fall under the pressure of all those expectations or self-administered expectations. It's one thing to talk about society but I think we also have to talk about the fact that a lot of our woes are about the stories we are telling ourselves about who we should be. There were lots of poems about motherhood, about the body, and these are very fraught topics for people because of all the ways we're told to do those things correctly: there's a *right* way to be a mother, there's a *right* way to have a body, there's a *right* way for a body to look. It's really interesting to talk about not just the moments of—yes, I have reclaimed motherhood—or—yes I've reclaimed my body and I'm proud of what it is—but also those moments that I feel like I'm failing, I feel like I'm falling, because I think those are unfortunately far more true to most people's experience. I think the poems that touched on that conflict were also some of the most remarkable.

AK: Interestingly you can't get away from the system of social control. You have a couple of choices, and the poems really show these choices well. There's one choice: which is to say—traditional female activities or behaviours have been devalued, and we are reclaiming the values of those activities—it's motherhood, it's caring, we are showing the heroism and we are proving that these should not be devalued. That's reaction one, but it is still identifying with the traditional compliant or feminine stereotypes, if you want. The other one is to say—fuck all this, I'm gonna get into the room that I'm locked out of. I'm badder than the guys or I'm better than the people in power, I'm gonna get in there and, through my achievement, conquer that territory that I've been excluded from.

15

VK: And it's the notion that the thing in the box is worth having.

AK: Exactly. And it still doesn't interrogate why the people in the room are in the room. It's focused on—I'm going to work to get into that room of power—so it's still a reaction to the system. And the third type of poem that was interesting is the witchiness. Here are people that historically were subversive, criminal, marginalised. Let's celebrate these figures as heroes of resistance against the system. And the problem for them of course is that yeah, they were fighters, but they're still dead, right? Oftentimes, we're still killed by the system and it goes back to what we said about the trade off, the cost, and the tiredness. And all of these different options are still reactions. You can never *not* react. You're always in that prism, the mental framework, so it's very difficult for any human to find true freedom.

VK: What I really loved about the pieces that we ended up choosing, what always struck me in a poem and made me want to look at it again, was when there was that complexity of relationship. I think it's so easy with a prompt like this to just talk about how much you revere a woman, whether she be Frida Kahlo or your grandmother, and write something very sweet and honouring, like—oh, this woman is amazing. Look at what she's achieved despite everything. But for me the true way to honour someone is to honour their complexity, the ugly moments, the parts of them that you found confounding or frustrating, allow women to be their full selves. I think this happens when you are talking about marginalised people: sometimes in an attempt to bring them up from their lowly place in the hierarchy of society, we turn them into deities, and you see it a lot when we talk about women. Even the notion of a Bad Betty is kind of in the same lexicon of *Yas Queen, goddess, amazing* and sometimes it's the time for that. But I think the poems that really stood out didn't fall into blind worship. They talked about women as they are.

AK: Being on the pedestal is a different kind of cage. We know that women have been put into these two categories: the Madonna or the whore. You could be the saint on the pedestal, or you could be the outcast, but you are not seen as a full spectrum human.

VK: Absolutely and people want the sort of messy, arty, unruly image of certain women, but in a sanitised, commodified way. I think a lot about the way people use the image of Frida Kahlo, how we are so used to seeing her image everywhere. And oftentimes people will get rid of her monobrow, and they will prettify her, and I do think there is something about the removal of her from her art, and the creation of her into a pop icon or pop figure, that speaks a lot about how we have commodified feminism in the most recent iteration of it. And so with this notion of a Bad Betty, I wanted to make sure that we got under the skin of it.

AK: Many Bond-type movies have some female physicist who is 21 years old, in a bikini, fixing a thermonuclear missile. These are not real people. It's another kind of tokenism, the same booby Barbie Bond girl of the early movies, only now she's also a theoretical physicist.

VK: And I think the 'Bad Betty' title is quite deceptive because it could so easily fall into these traps. But what you and I tried to do was pick poems that acknowledge the baggage of the title but also go underneath it and try to expand the notions of what that might mean. We have pieces like Laurie Bolger's 'Nanny Cis' which is short and sweet. And then we have more uncomfortable pieces, like Claudine Toutoungi's 'The Substitutes', where she goes through all these different mother figures, and then finally comes to her own mother, who says *Where have you been?* That acknowledgement that we can admire these women in our lives and also neglect them.

In a lot of the poems, the people written about were only seen as Bad Betties in hindsight, whether because the person passed away, or enough time had gone by, or someone had children themselves and then looked at their own mother with a whole new perspective. I love the self reflection that came with poems that were ostensibly about other people. It was really moving to see.

AK: I also really liked, for example, 'Ophelia's Swimming Lessons' by Chloe Bettles, because she's such a 'no-good subversive', but by giving her the name of Ophelia, and through the description, you get at that fragility and the cost of that revolt. As bad as Ophelia is, when you read the poem, you do worry about her. You worry about the cost to others, but also very much to herself.

VK: And these things reveal themselves on multiple readings. I liked the poems that reward readings, it's really exciting when poems have that ability to surprise you.

AK: I also really liked the poems that went beyond the individual Bad Betty, that created a kind of community of Betties, like 'this till is now closed' by Erdem Avsar. I saw this group of three people: each of them, in a way, a Bad Betty, and how they were connected tenuously and yet, so importantly to each other. This idea of a community and that some Bad Betties are fighting for someone other than themselves, bringing others along.

VK: I also want to talk about playfulness. There are lots of pieces that are more contemplative, some are quite heavy, so it was really important for me that we also had pieces that were fun, that have a little wink at the reader.

AK: And there's that in the concept of a Bad Betty, she does get to have a bit of fun.

VK: Humour is everything, right? Once you have people laughing, then you have their heart and you can take them to some darker places because there's trust there. So I really believe in humour as a means to get people to think about more serious issues. I'm really proud of us for getting such variety. It did mean that we had to let go of some wonderful poems, to make sure the experience of the book goes to so many different corners of what a Bad Betty might be.

AK: So, are we Bad Betties?

VK: Oh god, yeah. That's why we're here, baby.

THE HEXENHAUS INSIDE YOU

Flying Fish
Barbados, 1813

i was snipping off fins when muh water broke
dere are too many bones in us to be breeding
we should be more fish   buss out babies easier
dere will never be a *thank you* so why not grow scales
less painful   a reason fuh water
as i clenched muh teeth i noticed its mouth wide & ready
     i wanted to finish scraping its belly
          it needed to know it was dead

muh daughter arrived   sleeping   mouth shut
doing whatever de hell she wanted   covered in belly
her gran gran hung her upside down
smacked her boxcy   i heard her cry
i wanted to tell her what she knew was coming wasn't
dere are too many brains fuh us to be doing de same ting
but we do it   we work   we breed
remember de difference between living & not

i never finished soaking muh peas
i might just pretend to sleep so i don't have to
today a cock is being erected in St Michael   a thank you
fuh saving lives   his   i begat one   aunty begat three
so where de ass is we statue?

i never finished chopping off its tail   its mouth was too grateful
if it did survive perhaps i can borrow a fisherman's hook
hide it in muh basket   take a trip to town   swing at de statue
bag de Lord up in quarter pounds
sell he at market or exchange he fuh more fish

I, Temperance
(hanging)

I wish they all had but one body, so that we could burn them
all at once, in one fire! —Henri Boguet, *Discours des Sorciers*

Sometimes the only thing left to be built
is a funeral pyre.

We'll lift the wood together, bite the fruit,
remove our skins to watch

as they burn, curling around the edges.
We are the offerings.

Did you know Persephone chose to bite?
The red juice is all hers

as it spills between her teeth, runs the length
of her chin, shining red

marking her face with carnivorous fangs.
We all have some of those

although they mostly hide inside our gums
where we cannot feel them.

It's time for you to lose your fear of flames.
Time to embrace the smoke.

CHARLOTTE NEWBURY

Open up the Hexenhaus inside you,
let all your witches out

and don your new skin, feathered, ridged, warm as
hell in springtime. Costumed

in our own kind of armour. Bare your skull,
let the wind whistle through.

Fear not, my dear, they cannot kill us all.
They cannot kill us all.

My Grandma Tells Me She's Used a Darning Needle to Reach the Blackhead on Her Shoulder

the best way to eat currants is to hide them under your tongue
to re-hydrate a while

let your body patiently coax a little life back into them,

the soft muscle is the key - the tastiest meat comes
from closest to the bone

and remember this when you're hurting,

you can nurture a little pain but most must go
there is a way

to unpick even the difficult stitches, to make do,

focus and hold the needle just so, and with the angle all right
it's like being young

and able to wrap arms around yourself again,

she says *listen, listen* and it means *I have found another way
to make life a little sweeter*

to give you the tastiest snack, the longest reach.

To 木蘭

Somewhere under Mao's rubble, your bones are dirt.
Maybe magnolias grow where you lay,

your namesake shooting pink into the ground.
They're still telling your story like it's straight.

They want you bandaged in that pink dress, that short hair.
They want you running dirty from tree to pond.

They say you went home, swapped sword for pins,
bound mouth, not chest. I don't believe them.

Men have plucked blossoms and told me I was one, too,
said *look how hands snap pink into blue.*

But 姐姐, our lineage is older than bees.
There's always been more than one way to grow.

木蘭 /muk-laan/ Mulan; magnolia
姐姐 /jeh-jé/ older sister; term of address for a woman slightly
older than the speaker

extract from 'witchknot'

Arthur's leading a tournament next week
and I cannot be arsed with hosting
three dozen drunks and their sad servants
finding corners of the castle to touch one another

so much mead so many dead
things in the kitchen
I could have my pick
but I just can't be bothered

I've been getting into solo walks
helps me sort through thoughts
sometimes I see Morgan out
and I never know what she's up to

I wonder if she's got her eye on any knights
maybe Percival?
she'd crush him like lavender in her palm
or Lancelot?

something charming about him
despite the sexually aggressive name
I'm sure I'd think so
if I didn't feel so out of sorts

*

I see Morgan in the dining hall one morning
juggling apples like there's no tomorrow
my favourite way to break fast
is meat meat meat

Morgan is a fruit
lover which is to say
when she eats
you want to watch

I'm not sure if she's seen me
hiding on the threshold
she's staring into the distance
then as if a thread has been cut

she stops the juggle
and catches a green fruit
between her yellow teeth
a sound like bones breaking

*

there is some kind of kerfuffle
at the Round Table
a challenger to Lancelot has sought him out
for a post-breakfast duel

HELEN BOWELL

I think better to go at it before food
so if your entrails get spilled
it's less embarrassing
but whatever

this challenger's at the table with us
eating fried eggs
with those grease-lips
he's not even half as hot as Lance

why is he here Caelia whispers
Lancelot's fucked someone else's wife
again but Elaine heard
it was a family thing

land and honour
all the same if you ask me
nothing worth getting
your sausages in a twist about

*

couldn't sleep again last night
Arthur log-like beside me
and our maids snoring again
then a shadow outside

Merlin muttering pacing
I snuck out
summer lets you do such things
and he was kicking some ferns

of course he sensed me
trying to get good at sneaking out
are you he called
well sneak past this

and he threw a giant fern leaf at me
with ridges like fangs
it dropped to the ground
too light to travel

well done he said
and skulked away
sometimes I wish
I knew how

to unclench those shoulders
but Merlin doesn't respond well
to help or compassion
or other people

*

obviously I don't make this public knowledge
but I have fucked other people
than Arthur Pendragon
and I know a thing or two

I have tried imparting my wisdom
but to be honest
he doesn't seem overly interested
in developing his craft

*

this afternoon Morgan tells me
I could learn magic too
apparently my name means
The White Enchantress

which to be honest
I'm not that surprised about
she thinks that means
magic's in my blood

holding my hand
she asks about my parentage
the family skeletons
nothing to tell

she says we must try
and asks me to meet her on the edge
of the woods this Sunday midday
I just don't know what to wear

The Spanish Maids

It's the fashion to have a Spanish maid now.
All the bourgeoisie had a Carmen, Maria, Pilar, Teresa,
Concha, or Dolores at home. They didn't care whether

we came from Santander, Segovia, Salamanca or Zaragoza.
We lived at the top of the Hausmannian buildings tourists admire.
We had no running water, no bathroom, and squat toilets

that were often blocked and less often fixed.
My mistress sometimes received friends at home to play bridge.
While I was preparing coffee, I heard her say things like

She's very clean for a Spaniard, and she doesn't steal.
She tried to correct my accent in front of them,
cursed me for *speaking like a snake.*

When she was away, I opened wide the window overlooking
the courtyard and called the girls, so we could chat
and encourage each other while cleaning.

Sunday was our only day off: we went to mass together.
The French stared at us because we wore mantillas,
a sea of black lace cascading on our shoulders.

We sent money back home for our husbands to build
magnificent houses and for our children to go to school.
We'd planned to stay no more than ten or fifteen years.

ELLORA SUTTON

In a Dream Leonora Carrington Gives Me a Makeover

You are a debutante, she tells me.
Her hair floats behind her in thick snakes of smoke.
They are throwing a ball in your honour
and it will be awful. Something has to be done.

The rocking horse creaks and dreams of the open window. The window
is a cake of lemon-yellow curtains. It is hot like a real horse between my
legs. I only agreed to this because I am hungry and French isn't enough
anymore.

She does my eyes with a scalpel or a mongoose-hair paintbrush.
The moon is neighing like a blue violin.

There's no mirror so she carries me,
like a candle, to the window. I tell her
I think she's got my mouth all wrong.

Oh   do girls not have fangs?

She sighs a wimple into the cool air
and unhooks my face like a dress.
I swallow it whole. My face

is delicious. My true face, my gorgeous snout, my mongrel spots. She hands me an exquisitely embroidered clutch. Fleur-de-lis. And inside – my own old feet! pressed together like two vapidly dead holy white birds. My six swollen teats tumble from the taffeta, leaking. I am streaming. My four legs shake. My mouth knows only the shapes of laughter and flesh.

There, says Leonora Carrington, *my sweet hyena, isn't that better?*

Didn't I promise you

you would be well fed?

MARGUERITE HARROLD

The Legend of the Jars: Part 2

Momma liked her coffee black and room temperature
She liked her men hot and full of sugar
Momma liked her men

When the sun sagged below the Mangrove trees
Casting shadows on the wings of flies
She took her coffee from my hands

When in the mood
She told me stories about men
Who filled her purse with treasure

She brought home green backs
Jewels and foreign coins
And sometimes exotic women

Once she brought a man's ring that wore a finger
She *said* she found it by the pier
She said it didn't belong to anyone anymore

She pawned the ring but kept the finger
Bought dresses hats and gloves to match
Bought a cut glass jar for the finger
She said it would all belong to me one day

I THINK YOU SAVED MY LIFE

Last Rite: Ain't Much of a Life, She Says
after Kerri Arsenault

everything i write, is a way of saying: look,		i know this silence.
i am trying to tell you:

i know this voice. my mother is a simple poem		with a vast memory.
if you are asking yourself

if my mother is truly a small allotment of beauty		in the book of my life
you are both correct & asking

the wrong question. maybe my mother is a river.		maybe there is no limit
to what i can do with her name.

o black mother, o privy mother of the *Sunday's*		*best*—mother whose
song wakes the living—

rhapsody of the morning rise. i want more of it—		your hands, a gardenia
that survives me from the brambles

of old hurts—the choppy waters of our heritage.		i swore to myself i
would never write a bad poem.

i would never let anyone see the part of me		that trembles and moans
inside my hot and slow heart

let's be clear i hate goodbyes—hate its panic.		it's been 4 years' now
and i keep coming back to this small scale

OJO TAIYE

plot—an old ground where her seed is a western   expansion of gravity.
there is something paean

about prayer: my father wigged in a pool of   sorrow dreams he can
save my mother from dying

slowly of lung cancer. his arms around her   waist—she is weak and
having trouble sleeping—

a body suffering from the indignity of   a catheter. i say to my only
sister: i am having a bad day,

& her mood plummets. so much of loss   is love, so much of need is
a knotted hand hoping to *light*

everything we had to lose. which of her jokes   was best—*the Good Book*
of Ijapa, this exaltation of the tortoise's

shrewdness, a kind of missing cupped with   the abundance of tulips.
on the other side of the night

a childhood sweeter than tacos more holy   than the psalms of grief
all the complicated details of living

and the other side of the world becomes   too vague at my mother's
feet. i don't think there's any room

in the language for a lifetime of *crossing*.   if nothing my mother never
wanted to leave or sleep in the cold.

Mama Koko

how else to eat my own reflections? all along,
my night swells with the melodies of her oldest
laughter. we sing its blood, my avalanche—
there is a tenderness that follows language.
that winter, barely naked, she walks across the
acre as gently as she could, breathless, holding
cassava stems. her hands marked with welts, the
sharp-edged stanchion of hard labor. she's in love
with her occupation, her hayfield which reminds
me of lineage & dexterity. i think of her as living
her whole life wearing a red dress, spun outside in.
i can't remember a time there wasn't the constant
plop, plop from the cassava puree tied in a white
sack fermenting against the kitchen wall, or the
restlessness of squirrels gathering acorns at her
backyard. *my grandmother* balances her rounded
weight on a wooden stool, her voice hoarse & gold
even when she breaks melons. like braided cornrows,
the harmonies come out in timed measures. her head
raised high, staying attune to the bleating sound of goats
& sheep returning home to roost. as a child i would wrap
myself around her, & fall asleep while watching the moon
make magic of her tortoise tales—i mean beautiful nativity
stories, full of kinship & wisdom, the relics of a good god
whose name—shining & vaselined, wild & sweet drips
juice into my mouth like wonder.

Emma, Hannah,

my dearest bitches.
Look at you, Emma,
out at sea. And you, Hannah,
on site in high-vis.

My lady of cuttlefish,
my lady of brick dust,
what is your weather like?

These sandy home paths
still hold our footprints
from when we were six-legged
and the sky reeked so fresh.

My May Queens, my gorgeous cunts,

have I ever thanked you
for all the times I exploded
and you spent millennia
picking each disparate fragment of bone
      like wild strawberries
from the heather?

Interview (1)

Amy Winehouse sits in a black leather chair and looks at me calmly. She holds a naughtiness in her eyes, like she's daring me to do something fantastic. I trip over my words, slurring them, as they fight against one another to be free of my mouth.

I tell her I once watched a recording of her performing in a small church in Ireland.

I tell her my three favourite songs:

> You know I'm no good

> What is it about men?

> Love is a losing game

I say I saw a tribute band perform her album, *Frank*, in Belgrave Music Hall once. It was magical. The way I closed my eyes, the inside of my lids a promise of her presence. The way the crowd, dark shadows, moved like a freed cult, our bodies as one, pulsing black holes, the opening of a saxophone. The grit we felt between our teeth, white salt, the smell of damp and metal in the air. The lights, how they flashed, strobing moments, vultures feasting. My body, its twists, the way the grooves of my hips turned to silk when I heard her voice. That moment, in a dream, about to fall not knowing what you will catch as you do.

She is still for a moment, crossing and uncrossing her legs,
flicking her black hair over her shoulder. A silence as deep as
still water. She opens her mouth, just as I've started to speak
again. Our words mangle together, bashful and awkward.

I think you saved my life /

I never performed in a church

Someone here is lying.

this till is now closed

my Turkish mum had a long-distance relationship with Waitrose.
she loved Waitrose.
she would ring me every day and ask:

> **mum:** *gittin mi bugün o Waitrose'a?*
> *(did you go to that Waitrose place today?)*
> **me:** *yok anne, dolap dolu.*
> *(no mum, I've got everything in the fridge.)*
> **mum:** *yavrum yürü git bir bira al, Maryanne'le konuşursun.*
> *(go get yourself a beer darling, so you can have a chat*
> *with Maryanne.)*

this was my first year in Glasgow.
she wasn't trying to make me an alcoholic.
she just knew Maryanne would always ask for my ID for beer
      which meant leaving my student flat
              my Audre Lorde, my Judith Butler, and my Jasbir Puar
      which also meant speaking to an actual human being.

> **mum:** *ne dedi?*
> *(what did she say?)*
> **me:** *kim?*
> *(who?)*
> **mum:** *kimliğini sordu mu?*
> *(did Maryanne ask for your ID?)*
> **me:** *sordu.*
> *(she did.)*
> **mum:** *sen ne dedin?*
> *(what did you say?)*

me: *'ben 32 yaşındayım, iltifat olarak kabul ediyorum' dedim.*
              (I said: 'Oh, I'm flattered – I'm 32.')

mum: *sonra da 'ay valla bravo, ne yapıyorsan, aynen öyle devam*
              et' dedi?

              (and then she said 'wow, well-done, keep doing whatever
              you're doing'?)

me: *evet annecim. (yes mum.)*

mum: *sonra sen de 'genlerden herhalde, annem de çok genç gösterir'*
              dedin?

              (and then you said: 'must be the gene pool, my mum doesn't
              look her age either'?)

me: *evet annecim.*
              (yes mum.)

mum: *bir dahakine kasadayken telefonu kapatma, ben de duyayım*
              İngilizceni.

              (don't hang up next time you are at the tills, let me hear you
              speak English.)

she never met Maryanne, but she loved her
she was surprised to hear that a sixty-something woman
                could still flaunt a grey, tight hair bun
                wear an eyeliner that does not flake
                and remember a Turkish name after several ID checks.
beep
Maryanne scans a grapefruit soap bar
        after smelling it

maryanne: *this smells heavenly*
me: *I know! I'm so in love with it.*
mum: *ne diyor?*
              (what is she saying?)

me: *sabunu beğenmiş.*
              (that she likes the soap.)

mum: *nesi varmış sabunun? sor bi.*
              (what's so special about it? ask her.)

me: *annecim, şunları yerleştiriyorum, bir dur.*
              (mum, I'm bagging, could you please – just a minute.)
              I'm sorry.

maryanne: *please take your time Erdem.*

mum: *aa bak yine adını söyledi, ERR-DAM dedi.*
              (ha! she said your name again, she said ERR-DAM)

me: *öyle oldu annecim.*
              (yes, I think she did mum.)

beep
Maryanne scans the latest issue of Gay Times
     after checking out the sizzling Harry Judd on the cover

maryanne: *so, you've made it to the Gay Times*

me: *thanks, but I think he would be very offended*
              Maryanne

maryanne: *do you have things like these back home?*

me: *we have the angry, political, activist stuff*
              but perhaps not the celebrity, vegan food or bubble butt
              stuff.

mum: *Maryanne'e mi açıldın sen? gey mey dedi.*
              (did you just come out to Maryanne? she said gay)

me: *hayır annecim.*
              (no mum.)

mum: *hayret, buradayken tutamıyordun.*
              (that's strange, you couldn't help it when you were
              here.)

beep
Maryanne scans a bunch of pink peonies
        after gently caressing each petal and smelling her fingers.

mum:	*şimdi neyi geçirdi?*
	(what did she scan just now?)
me:	*şakayık annecim.*
	(peonies mum.)
mum:	*aa, annem çok sever de.*
	(aw, tell her that they're my favourite.)
maryanne:	*what is she saying?*
me:	*that they are her favourite.*
maryanne:	*she should come and see them for herself.*

my mum never managed to get a visa
pink peonies lasted for four weeks
I left the Gay Times on a bus
and the first term ended on a whim when I met Aidan from the queer
sexualities group
        who stood up
        after the group convener reminded me (every five minutes)
        the super obvious fact that
        I was the darkest in the group
        Aidan said some politically correct things about racialisation
        I don't remember what exactly
        I was too busy imagining the stache rash I would get from
        kissing him
after three rashes
I moved in with Aidan
he said it was super-super-super weird that I lived in the West End
and shopped at Waitrose with my less than minimum wage stipend

I didn't say it was because I was terribly-terribly-terribly lonely
I wanted to be the independent exotic queer
            not the immigrant loser queer
Southside was affordable and hipstery,
we shopped at Asda and Lidl
and I soon forgot about Maryanne.

1 missed call from mum

as I spent two years with Aidan and his gang
my mum was relieved that I had someone

1 missed call from mum

though the rushed romance between our cut and uncut dicks

mum missed your call

had ended after two months

2 missed calls from mum

when he told his queer Marxist pals
(during a heated discussion on how to dismantle the rhetoric of
dismantling) how happy he was
because he made me the activist I turned out to be

mum missed your call

but thanks to a self-centred apology and not having sex anymore
we remained friends

1 missed call from mum

my mum didn't mind Aidan

mum, incoming call, 67 minutes, 32 seconds

but she would be happy to hear that he drove me to the airport

mum missed your call

and that he didn't object to stopping at the Waitrose in the West End

mum missed your call
mum missed your call
mum missed your call

when I said:

me: *my mum died.*

that was the last time I saw Maryanne
at the same till point
looking exactly like she looked three years ago.

beep
Maryanne scans four cans of Innis & Gunn

maryanne: *can I please see your ID... ERRR-DAM?*

she smiles.
I smile.

maryanne: *call your mum, I'll say hi.*

I show her the long list of missed calls.

me: *brain tumor.*

I sort of expect her to tear up
but she doesn't
she tightens her sock bun as if to check if it is still there
she looks to see if there is a grunting, angry queue behind me.
there is.
she shouts:

maryanne: *this till is now closed.*

she leaves, as gently as always, and without hurry.
and comes back with the latest issue of Gay Times with Ncuti
Gatwa on the cover
and a bunch of pink peonies.

Football Food in Silesia
for Jana

We went back to your Osciedle
Overlooking the Polish, Irish bar
And the Polish, Italian place
And the Polish, Chinese place
Where we drank with other expats
Over fusion fried-rice-lasagne

We went back to your Osciedle
Where you hosted us on game nights
With white chicken chilli
Or bacon mac and cheese
With improvised ingredients
Picked up from biedronka

We went back to your Osciedle
And I laughed at your food photos
Which were always too close
And lit far too bright
And did no justice
To your skills in the kitchen

I go back to your Osciedle
In my mind, each time I cook
With improvised ingredients
Recipes I wish I asked for
These meals feel too far, too dark
And I cannot do justice to you

Ayaan bunks History and sits next to me in Art

It's important to note that throughout double Art,
Ms Dicks didn't realise she had an extra student.
In a few years' time, we will wonder if she was racist
for not being able to tell any of us apart.
We will wonder if all of our teachers were racist.
In this specific lesson, Ayaan sits next to me
looking confused. She sees the whiteboard
covered with stains of paint shaped like fingerprints,
coloured water never cleaned off. She turns
and sees my sketch of a Matisse impression.
Is this it? She asks, *You just sit here and draw for your A*?*
Following a dead white man's definition of art
while I have to learn about other dead white
men and their definition of peace.

Best women, I miss you

plus recipes, takeaways, shit telly,
lightweight parcels with biro stars
and hearts, pet names of unknown
origin, *FishyEm, Peanut, Scraps,* our
giggling stops sleep, *the next one to*
make noise is a poohead and that's that,
urging each other not to spend our
hot glowing energies on the wrong
damn things, pooling resources for
decent birthday presents, discussing
the same fraught nonsense over over
over 'til it makes us ill, gnawing at old
problems, picked clean, analysed dead,
yelping at the text that tells me you left
him, infinite stream of prosexxy at that
hot tub hen party, fried eggs, mountain
walks in fine Welsh rain, *why weren't you*
there? sobbing into Thai green curry and
prawn toast, heartbreak croissants, your
voice notes unspooling in my lonely ear,
she was honestly about to pop, shit that's my bus
giving wise advice, not taking it, dropping
mushy pea fritters splat on the chip shop
floor, scooping them up, *waste not want not*
into open gob, cue seaside disapproval,
please, please let's all get together, summoning
the longed for summer witch-like, *please*
love me forever, breaking the reservoir's
taut coin with our gooseskin bodies.

A new game
for Pauline Kwiat

Playing cards arranged face down   in three squares on your kitchen table

The walls are mustard yellow from when that was fashionable.   The baby is crying

in the next room   you tell me you're trying a new thing where you ignore her

for the first ten minutes.   Mike says   *I pick up games really quickly,*   we lift our eyes

at each other.   He catches us, blushes.   You complete our first round winning and smile

like a cat. I touch the actual cat and my eye reddens   bulging   an elephant's heart.

You fetch me an antihistamine   tell him off for drinking
all the good wine

not giving you or me   the guest!   a chance to catch up.

Mike wins round two and I'm enjoying losing, truly.

My battened down soul   now   open
        gentle   blinking.

I CAN BE A SHOW PONY

Ain't You a Peach

I can be a show pony
when I want a cash tip.
I know they think of me
in my tight jeans
when their quiet sons
eat potatoes.
I was a kid once.
I imagined a room
full of men in suits
ordering two fingers
of whiskey.
I touched myself
on a camp bed
in the dark.
To get to the room
you have to drive
down a long motorway
in a smoke-filled car.
You have to know
about motorways.
I'm a basic girl,
strawberry chapstick,
candles. Cheap green dresses.
Sometimes I'm flattered
when they shout from vans.
My cousin once pinned me
against the wall with
his mouth.

I had a hamster
and a CD player.
He arrived nervous
but his hands knew
how to slide a bolt.
I didn't give
but I stood still.
My auntie says
one day
the whistles will stop
and I'll miss them.
He's married now,
two boys.
Don't we all just want that
good night's sleep?

Girl Poets

The girl poets are unconvincingly heightened.
They are ground-breaking and important. It is a shame.
They live in un-assuming vignettes
fuzzy with new possibilities   intellectually
abstruse.   The girl poets could be in trouble.
The girl poets are not an idle concern.

Their poems were born in the rubbish tip   awkward
and misunderstood. Their poems are creatures
we can never approach   boxes of trinkets
          decorative and over-designed   crude
with sentimentality   like internet censorship.
Their best poems are double   faced.

The girl poets are lexicographal conjecture.
They are trivial   beasts   stalking themselves
down streets of dissenting cities   tailing
versified intelligence at the supermarket   aimed
and aimless   drawn by the superficial tingle
of their mildly irritating electric heat.

The girl poets are successful and very presentable.
Slight   brusque   tricky. They pummel
with chatty allusion   childlike. They bark.
They cannot be taken seriously   wearing
as they will   warm and woolly   restless
feelings   (like the best and worst of this style).

The girl poets live like they write   with charming
clumsiness   unconvincing   florid
with earnestness. It blooms   sixth-formy   from
their oblique and gracefully elaborate skin.
The girl poets are working harder   transformed
into soaring birds.   The girl poets win.

CHLOE BETTLES

Ophelia's Swimming Lessons

Ophelia brings tuna sandwiches to the picnic by the koi pond.

Ophelia tells you to 'watch this!' then doesn't do anything.

Ophelia gets voted most likely to succeed
because someone spread a rumour that she showed
boys her vagina in exchange for squeezy yogurts
after class. Even though she's lactose intolerant.
Even though she has a boyfriend from another school.

Ophelia would have done it if she thought of it first.

Ophelia can't drive but is going places.

Ophelia suggests you take the long way home
and cries when you get lost. Suggests the two
of you run away together because five minutes
past curfew is too late but not enough of a statement.
That the two of you deserve your own time zone.

Ophelia has a restraining order against herself.

Ophelia makes you keep her misery company.

Ophelia wants someone to name a hurricane after her.
Wants someone to chase her. Wants someone other
than you. But over time her storm gets downgraded
to a tropical depression that you tourist in, build
a rental spot in the scabs at the crook of her elbow.

CHLOE BETTLES

Ophelia is tanning oil over suntan lotion.

Ophelia suggests skinny-dipping but doesn't know how to swim.

Ophelia sticks her tongue down your throat
during mouth to mouth and laughs when you cry.
Lets you play make believe with her body
with kisses that taste exactly like pond water-
kisses that taste exactly like teething biscuits.

Ophelia takes your virginity and hides it.

Ophelia calls sex 'Bumping Uglies' and does it often.

Ophelia needs something warm between her thighs
to digest her food properly. Has a reoccurring dream
where she sheds her skin to the sound of trumpets.
Whispers gossip from behind her prayer book every
Sunday because she believes in Eve but not in God.

Ophelia reads her horoscope religiously.

Ophelia is compatible with fire.

Ophelia starts smoking to get more fresh air.
Starts hanging out with older guys.
Starts bringing you on double dates where
she cries choosing a lobster from the tank
but still wants the most expensive thing on the menu.

Ophelia asks you what loving her feels like.

Ophelia leaves love bites that can't be concealed.

Ophelia kisses you like she's trying to consume you–
like she could stomach you anyway.
Promises she'll never love you.
Promises she'll never leave you.
Yet she'll do both and never apologise for either.

Ophelia knows what outfit she wants to be buried in.

Ophelia doesn't look both ways.

Ophelia deletes her Facebook page an hour before her birthday
but still gets mad when no one but you remembers,
punches you in the middle of the lunch line,
then still wants to sit beside you in the headteacher's office
as you tell her you don't think you can do this anymore.

Ophelia picks the scabs off her knuckles and gives them to you.

Ophelia double knots your shoelaces and says, 'watch this.'

Ophelia swallows the waiting room goldfish as a distraction.

o to be liz taylor

to have a tongue i could shuck oysters with / to fuck and fight with relish /
to swear like a coal miner in a pub in port talbot / to be decked in bulgari
with a ship-launching face / to scandalise the vatican / to kick it with the
kennedys / to guide a rising star inside of me / to be a beautiful broad / to
enrage my two-time spouse on our million dollar yacht / to revel in their
explosions like i'm watching my own movie / to be shrill and sexy / to be
magnetically vulgar / to break my fast with bloody marys / to burn brighter
than the ingenues eyeing up my baby / to tell them out of spite how we rut
like rabbits / to be held aloft on a dais with togaed extras below me / to
know they'd been told to call out *Cleopatra* / to find them instead screaming
my name

Nanny Cis

She worked at the Coca Cola
factory for years —

always told us it was her
who put the fizz in those bottles.

JILL MICHELLE

I've Had My Fun
for Andrea (1973 – 1988)

Of course, we lowly sophomores got sixth-bell lunch. The last, most
Ravenous pack, we'd grab aluminum-wrapped chicken sandwiches
And soggy fries, snag a chocolate milk, if any remained, pay, then
Nestle beside our weighty backpacks, someone always scrambling to
Get seventh-bell's homework done while the rest of us play cards,
Eat, read, gossip. In 1988 we have no Facebook, no smart phones to

Check. We give and get our statuses in person—relationship updates
Relayed over mayo-mixed ketchup puddles, news and hopes discussed
Under the comforting buzz of a hundred other cafeteria conversations.
Sliding in late, my best friend feeds us details of her dermatologist visit,
Happily reports on the prescription, not knowing this is how her life ends.

Gertrude Stein, in conversation and as observed through a carafe

There is a cigarette and there is a lighting and I am tucking into bloody roast beef. Bloody roast beef is best served, best served, severed best red. The glass fills itself too eagerly and now there are stains on the tablecloth. Red can mean all these things and yet also mean none of them. It can be just red. Someone comes in to change the dining room portraits. Someone comes in to rearrange the chairs. Paris rolls back the window, rolls under the window, rolls over the window. Someone comes. Chokes. In another room, someone bangs a table. The paintbrush glass tips over. I say there is a difficulty of producing description which is solely engaged in the present. The paintbrush glass rights itself, writes itself, tap dances across the table and talks like a newshound about cubism. We draw cubes in the dust. We drink red wine wrung out from stained tablecloths, tableclothe ourselves in satin, best when wet. Someone serves coffee. The sugar is neglected. Gertrude tells me come back soon, tells me come back, come back. Come. I get trapped in the shutters. I get trapped in the doorway. I get trapped between flattery and falling. I fall asleep in Paris and wake up reading, wake up speaking, wake up writing. It is not the same.

BESEECH THE SKY

Hotel Service

I see a maid in Dakar gently close the door,
head bent towards her pregnant belly, straining
at the uniform, small stain on the front.

She's carrying a broom as if a walking stick,
shuffles down the corridor, half-asleep,
shadowed by dull light, a window she must clean.

Outside, the sun sets fire to the street.
Car horns blare, insisting they are stronger
than the call to Friday prayers. Men beseech the sky.

She taps the broom towards dim stairs, inhales
before she takes a step. Descends but has to stop.
Her back might give with six more flights of work –

to change rank sheets, pick up damp clothes.
Her pay is less than tourists spend on bags
of local weed, a can of lukewarm beer.

Down in the hotel bar – red lights, plush seats –
a fan whirs overhead, the Top Ten on repeat.
I sip a long, cool drink, write about the maid.

No longer these rays[1]

Then I feared clenched hands and blood
unopened, the beer bottle of the back of
childhood church, pastor's hand in my
back pocket taking the climate's shape.

We had nothing left but a strange
contiguity, overlapping in beds
flooding with shadows; these rays of
sunlight untouched all round us.

In my mind you are silhouetted by
playwrights asphyxiated in the lining
of their lovers' bodies, the offensive
one takes before an impasse.

Though in truth none of these are native
thoughts, they are the fears that belonged
to us, slouching towards bethlehem[2] in
the harsh summers of office rooms.

1| The title of this poem is a reference to *Delayed Rays of A Star*, a book by
Amanda Lee Koe.
2| *Slouching towards Bethlehem* is the title of a collection of essays by Joan
Didion, which takes its title from WB Yeats' poem 'The Second Coming'.

FEE GRIFFIN

What Keeps Me Going Is

I carry a photograph of Patti Smith in my lungs.
The photograph is one cell thick like the walls of blood capillaries
and has a large surface area.
I am careful not to breathe on Patti Smith.
I sing on short car journeys so the image of Patti Smith can see out.
The photograph of Patti Smith diffuses from a high concentration in my lungs
to a lower concentration in my red blood cells.
This is how substances move around our bodies.
The presence of the photograph betrays my childish idea of
the lungs as empty & operating like bagpipes;
In reality of course my tissues are fused with the Kodak paper.
I have been unable to breathe well since January.
A pale absence forms over areas of Patti Smith.
My heart compensates by beating too fast, my arms shake when I eat.
The chest x-ray is two weeks old
but I have not been called back by the doctor
who delays and delays, struggling to form her question.

Mother's Wisdom

(Inspired by my / mum, who speaks in crossword clues / and cryptic senryu)

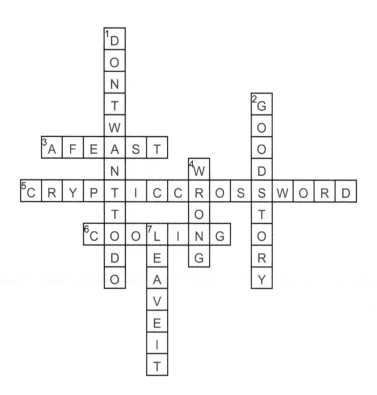

Across

3. Enough is as good as
5. Piecing together the conversation like a
6. Evaporation causes

Down

1. Never show an aptitude for things you
2. Never let the truth get in the way of a
4. A mother's place is in the
7. It's more of a waste to eat than to

Illness as Living For
for Susan Sontag

When we were children, our mothers fed us
gefilte fish, matzo, chicken soup, and latkes.

They gave us things to make us stronger.
When we had cancer, our doctors fed us

doxorubicin, a red drug, a trick, fake blood
that eventually breaks your heart.

It was hard. Someone gave me 'Illness
as Metaphor.' That was easy to read:

You read and you have cancer.
Also: *I think you think too much.*

So, I read your ideas without a body –
always, *cancer*, never, *mine*. Never, *I*.

I do think too much, about whether my heart
will stop beating before it starts loving.

At twenty-one, I wonder if it's easier to stop
if I've never started. But then I started

reading your diaries, and they opened me
up to it, to loving, to living for loving.

Your loves were a medicine for my guilt
which dissolved, with my cancer, into hope.

I hope I don't love her, became, I do – *I hope
she loves me.* In my childhood bed,

I hoped, and read 'Reborn' and was.
One day, *This.* Then, *No – this, this...*

This opening opened more opening, and soon
I was falling apart watching your lips

in an old video. You're angry at Norman Mailer
for saying *lady critic*, and you say *lady*

like *love*, like it means all the ladies
you have loved, all the secrets inside all the words

which were never *I*. I take those words and open them.
Doxorubicin and its rubies. They're everywhere,

those rubies – in our words, in our bodies, in our blood.
Break me apart, break me, I'll only open –

inside of me there is only more
to live for.

Nobody lives forever my teacher

reminds me every Sunday School class so
I just nod my head and if she says so
to me solely and nobody else then
I nod harder and say *Yes ma'am* and smile
and she smiles back and that's the death of it,
the end I should say, if she's at her desk
she opens her Bible back up, then I
say *Goodbye, ma'am—see you next Sunday* and
sometimes she looks up (and smiles) and says good
-bye and sometimes it's goodbye without look
-ing up and sometimes she doesn't seem to
hear me and sometimes she just smiles, she's torn
between me and the Good Book, I guess, so
I just leave like the ghost she's giving up.

GALE ACUFF

I'm bigger than Jesus I tell my Sun

-day School teacher after class today just
to see if I can rile her, it's revenge
at the heart of it because she took my
comic book from me while she was going
on about the Sermon on the Mount and
I like that part of the story, it's sure
a good one but I like Wonder Woman
more and she isn't even real but then
neither is God—it just came to me like
a revelation, during the Lord's Prayer
which she made me lead the class in and I
did without stumbling, I could say it back
-wards if I had to, but as for revenge
she laughed and sang *Goodbye—see you next time.*

CLAUDINE TOUTOUNGI

The Substitutes

All my alternative mothers line up in the courtyard to pass me along.
One picks lint from my coat. The next tuts at my shoes till a matron
from Tuscany pinches my cheek, crying *Cara! Carina! Cucciola!*
(confusing as none are my name). A woman in steel-rimmed spectacles
hands me *Das Kapital* and a language manual, *Deutsch Direkt,* which
I dump, coughing, as a twinset-and-pearls sprays me with clouds of
Chanel and I'm swivelling into a curlers-and-marigolds, who thrusts
a sink-plunger into my hands, insisting *I'm not Mrs Mop* and so
on and so forth: the rock chick who wants us to do some lines; a harpist
mummified in chiffon, who needs me to turn the page; the exec (remote
in a headset) drumming instructions to Infinite Loop; a meditating
yogi, complete with gong; and finally, very far off, I see her—my mother
billowing in a nightie, her beautiful face looking huffy and strained.
Where have you been? she asks when I reach her. *You've been ages.*
I've been waiting. Where have you been?

Acknowledgements

The Bad Betty Press team would like to express our gratitude for the time, talent and tenacity of this book's editors, Vanessa Kisuule and Anja Konig, who approached the curation of these poems with vigour, with humour, with nuance, with joy, with enquiry, and with wisdom. They truly are two of the baddest Betties we know.

We'd like to thank the twenty-five poets published in this book, who trusted us with their wonderful work, and each brought something unique and vital to the anthology.

We're grateful to illustrator Helen Nicholson, who created the beautiful cover for this book, and whom we're delighted to be working with again.

Thank you Clare Pollard and Joelle Taylor for the kind words.

Thank you Arts Council England for supporting our work and making this book possible.

And finally, to all the Bad Betties—those writing and those written about, those who inspire others and and those who go unseen, but continue fighting, surviving, working and loving: we salute you.